Everyone Can Drum!

By Corey Kertzie and Vinnie Amico

Illustrated by Fred Whitehead

Amelia

Press

Copyright © 2013 by Corey Kertzie and Vinnie Amico

Illustrations by Fred Whitehead

All rights reserved. No part of this publication may be reproduced, stored in a retrieval system, or transmitted, in any form or by any means, electronic, mechanical, photocopying, recording, or otherwise, without the written prior permission of the author.

Printed in the United States of America

Everyone Can Drum/ First Edition

ISBN: 978-0615812397

Amelia Press is an imprint of No Frills Buffalo
119 Dorchester
Buffalo, New York 14213
Visit Nofrillsbuffalo.com

From Vinnie

My dad for getting me interested in music.
My mom for getting me started.
My wife Deb and kids, Marley and Madison for their endless inspiration and support.
And to all those who have taught me along the way...

From Corey

To my beautiful wife Michele, for always telling me to do what makes me happy.
To my kids, Dylan and Alexa, who make me proud every day.
To my new niece, Addyson, and my new nephews, Aiden and Connor; May you always be in rhythm and have the musical flow of life.
To Jessica Topper, a beautiful person, both inside and out.
And to my wonderful family, who I am very fortunate to be a part of.

For drums to accompany this book contact:
Nathaniel Hall at Everyone's Drumming:
1-800-326-0726 or www.everyonesdrumming.com

Seeing a drum makes people HAPPY!

Playing a drum makes you feel GREAT!

Everyone Can Drum.
There is a drummer in everybody,
And in every body there is a **DRUM!**
Put your hand on your heart,
feel your heartbeat,
this is your body's drum.

Your heart beats in a **rhythm (ri-thum)**.
A rhythm is a sound in a pattern.

Your body works in rhythm. Listen to your footsteps as you walk, they make a rhythm.

The world is full of rhythms. Close your eyes and listen for rhythms all around you.

As you do, count along with them.

1 - 2 - 3 - 4   1 - 2 - 3 - 4

Once you learn to count with the different rhythms, you can learn to make them on your own.

If you will learn to keep them even and in time, YOU will be a great DRUMMER!

Now you are on your way!

Drums come from all over the world. At first they were made from wood and animal skin. These come from the earth. The skin fits tight around the drum shell. This skin is called the drum head. When the drum is hit, it makes a sound vibration.

Drums can be played with your hands or a stick. When you hit the drum, it makes a vibration.

Just like your eardrum!

As you hit the drum, make sure you let your hand or stick bounce off of the drumhead. Learn to "feel" the drum.

The sound a drum makes is called the tone. Different drums have different tones. Big drums have a low deep tone and smaller drums have higher tones. You can tune your drums to get different tones. If you tighten the drumhead you will get a higher tone, if you loosen it, the tone will be lower. Using a stick will also give you a different tone than if you use your hand. Now, try it yourself to hear the different tones.

It's fun to learn rhythm with other people. Get Dad, Mom, Brother, Sister or some of your friends together. Sit in a circle and give them all something to play.

You can add sounds
by playing on pots or pans...
even a garbage can or
plastic pail if you want!

For another fun sound, take an empty plastic spice bottle and fill it with rice or popcorn kernels. Now shake it. Now you have another great rhythm sound: a shaker.

What else can you use to make drum sounds?

If there aren't enough things for people to play, you can just clap your hands.

Here's an easy rhythm to start with.
Hey...hey...you...you...1 and 2...1 and 2...

Hear...hear...the...the...drum...drum...sound...sound
Try only to clap on the 1 and 2

1 - 2 - 3 - 4   1 - 2 - 3 - 4
(clap) (clap)   (clap) (clap)

Now try it on a drum
Keep repeating it and you have a rhythm!

For fun, start out beating the drum slowly, then get faster and faster and faster. So fast, until you can't go any faster! Count to 4 out loud, and stop

Wow! That was great...wasn't it?

Rhythms can be played at different speeds. This is called Tempo. You can speed up a tempo or slow it down if you want.

Just remember to keep the rhythm even.

Switch instruments with the person next to you, so everyone can learn a different part of the rhythm.

The drum can be played loud or soft. This is called dynamics.

Once you get the hang of rhythm and dynamics, you will be able to play any drum
and the world has plenty of different drums to choose from!

.

In Latin America they play Congas and Bongos

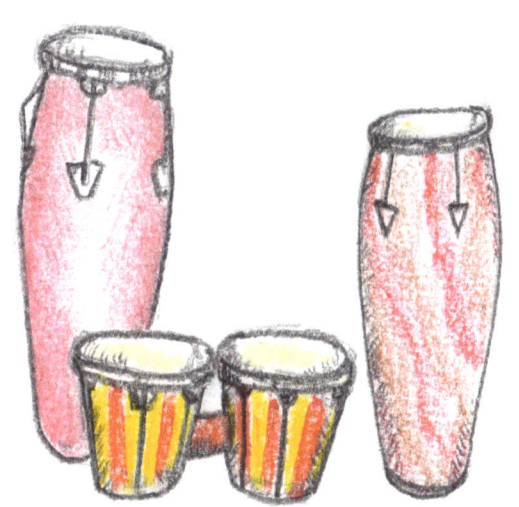

In India the drums are called Tablas. They look like Bongos but have a very different sound.

Some drums from Africa are called Djembes or Ahikos.

In America we combine drums to make a drum set. This has a bass drum, snare drum, tom-tom drums and cymbals.

Many cultures around the world used drums to talk to one another over long distances. Some still do.

By learning rhythm and tempo,
you too can learn the language of drumming!

Follow the lessons on the next few pages. Use different instruments and invite your friends to join in.

Have Fun!

We are all drummers in our own way, and don't even know it! Our lives and the world move together in rhythm, being aware of these rhythms, feeling and hearing them. Using them and practicing them can make you a great drummer.

See, everyone can drum!
Now try these rhythms!

Rhythm 1

1 - 2 - 3 - 4 / 1 - 2 - 3 - 4
clap   clap   clap   clap   clap   clap

1 - 2 - 3 - 4 / 1 - 2 - 3- 4
clap   clap   clap   clap   clap   clap

Rhythm 2

1 - 2 - 3 - 4 / 1 - 2 - 3 - 4
clap   clap   drum   drum   clap   clap   drum   drum

1 - 2 - 3 - 4 / 1 - 2 - 3 - 4
clap   clap   drum   drum   clap   clap   drum   drum

Rhythm 3

1 - 2 - 3 - 4 / 1 - 2 - 3 - 4
clap   clap   drum   drum   stomp   stomp   clap   clap

1 - 2 - 3 - 4 / 1 - 2 - 3 - 4
pan   pan   shaker   drum   shaker   drum

Rhythm 4

1 - 2 - 3 - 4 / 1 - 2 - 3 - 4
clap clap   clap   clap

1 - 2 - 3 - 4 / 1 - 2 - 3 - 4
          drum   drum   drum   drum

Rhythm 5

1 - 2 - 3 - 4 / 1 - 2 - 3 - 4
drum drum drum   drum drum drum

1 - 2 - 3 - 4 / 1 - 2 - 3 - 4
drum drum drum   drum drum drum

Rhythm 6

1 - 2 - 3 - 4 / 1 - 2 - 3 - 4
drum   drum   drum   drum

1 - 2 - 3 - 4 / 1 - 2 - 3 - 4
drum   drum   drum   drum

Rhythm 7

1 - 2 - 3 - 4 / 1 - 2 - 3 - 4
drum   drum drum   drum

1 - 2 - 3 - 4 / 1 - 2 - 3 - 4
drum   drum drum   drum

Now create your own!

1 - 2 - 3 - 4 / 1 - 2 - 3 - 4

1 - 2 - 3 - 4 / 1 - 2 - 3 - 4

1 - 2 - 3 - 4 / 1 - 2 - 3 - 4

1 - 2 - 3 - 4 / 1 - 2 - 3 - 4

1 - 2 - 3 - 4 / 1 - 2 - 3 - 4

1 - 2 - 3 - 4 / 1 - 2 - 3 - 4

About the Authors

From Western NY, co-author Corey Kertzie is a drummer with over 35 years of experience, as well as an artist, a husband, and father of two. Writing a children's book has always been something he has wanted to do because of his love for teaching children and opening up their creative minds. What better topic than something he has extreme passion for: drums. Corey is known for his blend of drumming and percussion from all over the world; his book tells children about them all.

Currently performing with Big Leg Emma, Corey is known as the heart of some of the best bands around. His roots stem back to his days of double drumming with the book's co-author, Vinnie Amico, for over seven years. It was only recently that the two returned to their partnership. Although not drumming physically together these days, they are bringing to life the rhythm and sounds that surround us every day, and putting them into the hearts and minds of children everywhere.

Everyone Can Drum is an interactive educational book about drumming around the world, but written to be fun and engaging for all who open it. We hope you enjoy our creation, and it opens the doors to bring music into your child's life.

Vinnie became interested in music at a very young age, as his dad was a professional trumpet player...He grew up listening to jazz music. Vinnie started playing the drums at the age of ten and was playing professionally by the age of 18. Vinnie has made a career out of playing drums since 1996 when he started playing with the popular rock/jam band moe. He is still playing with moe. today as well as many other projects. "I am very interested in getting children started in music early and sharing my knowledge to get everyone to drum. I hope you like our book."

www.ingramcontent.com/pod-product-compliance
Lightning Source LLC
Chambersburg PA
CBHW041542040426
42446CB00002B/194